Somnata

By
Donavon Davidson

For
Aodhán

Acknowledgements

Thank you to my family and friends who, without their support and understanding, this collection would not be possible.

"I want to sleep the sleep of the apples"

from Gacela of the Dark Death

-Federico Garcia Lorca

I

Nothing can be done
When you break the earth
You take it apart
And it is not what it was
Because you are like nothing
Because you are like nothing
You take it apart
With a loving shadow
That darkens those daisy eyes
That is their shelter of wings
That is your shoulder of night

With the sounds of chains falling
You come together
With incredible wings, and
Crowd heavens hour
And calm falls in the immense
Shadow of your flock
Watching the children
Abandon nothing
That one day they will forget
And so put it together
To see themselves in a wheel

When you let them all your dreams
That only hurts a little
You borrow the wing
Of a child who had lost it
By putting it together
Inside the house of summer
Placing the sun in its house
And went on living
Inside the wheel of a clock
Setting people on fire
For an artificial night

Because you were born
I have two shadows
One that lives inside a cloud
Where there is no peace
Free from what I understand
A mysterious trace
That does not come out of me
Yet, only by me
Walking along as I walk
I imagine that you know
I will never see again
So you put it together
And I fall apart

Smaller, I will tell my ghost
You will remember
You will remember
Nothing when you wake
So go to sleep my angel
This is no place for seeing
Not while you gather the sky
Pinned up behind your shoulder

Because you are young
And you carry so little
Do not look on me
As you would mirrors
That do not notice
The waking hour
Is a flight of opened eyes
Heavens meteor
With its hollow mouth
Bringing suicide
To even the most
Innocent daisies
Do not look on me
I know where you go
And what it means to forget
And fly away from the house
And call to the sun

The sound of black birds
Calling through the sun
Is the sound the spirit makes
Caught between two worlds
It is a tearing away
It is a tearing away
When something so fragile hurts
This is the sound of the night
Coming together
It is a tearing away

When I was passing
I felt the wheel rub its hands
Timing the cloud break
And the opened egg
Every nest waited
For a rain to fall
And so the day would begin
Neither sleeping or awake
There was nothing left in me
I was almost too fragile
For even the light to block
My skin was calling
For the little trace
Left in my shoulders
Overwhelming dream
It hurt to be seen
Fading like I was
No one could look on me
Without some fear of themselves
Hoping for my death

I look away from faces
Half blind and half full of wings
Unable to live or die
I'm afraid I'll see through them
So I look away
Unable to live or die
Half blind and half full of wings
I look away from faces

Dreams are born in the shadow
In the million wings of night
Sent down and weeping
Gentle as the dew
A small child stirring from sleep
The sudden face of stopped clocks

The sun rang its bell
And night divided its wings
Among the living
Terrible sounds of hunger
Had gone unnoticed
Or unrecognized
Because they were so pretty
Moving as you move

Some will fall in love
Because they are like nothing
Trying to take it apart
Finally breaking the earth
And give up dreaming
Trying to take it apart
Because they are like nothing
Some will fall in love

You have passed through eyes
Before they opened
Blisters in the sun
And let down your wing's
Arrest by final hour
And let him your hands
Cut loose from its string
And then fell apart
Giving me your dreams
To watch over you

The sound of a house
Somewhere in the sky
Opens and closes
The gang of wanting
In a daisy's eye
When the time is right
Snowflakes will fall from the sky
Smaller than a dream
Sending flowers to seasons
And wind those darlings
Somewhere in the earth
In place of shadows
Black and flightless birds
Will come together
That is a sound a house makes
Half earth and half flying dream
When you call for me

You never go when you leave
You have a living in you
That seems to torment
And then take the breath away
That is my other shadow
That only tells what's been done
Nothing can be done
With a list of strings
Hopeless for your love
Nothing can be done with me
When I read this list

The night must be wings
Tearing away into sleep
For those passing through
It isn't the same
Showing the hour its wheel
For those passing through
Tearing away into sleep
The night must be wings

I want you to know
I think about you, right now
When you are still young
Before you come together
And give your name to the wind
That it might call me
And remember you
As if you were lost
But you'll never know
You will never know
I think about you, right now
When you are still young

II

If you visit me
With heavy colors
Make it all the pretty ones
I want to understand you
With a black face on your arm
With gentle hooks in your eyes
With wounded astrologies
If you come for me
Hold on to the haunting snow
Now that you know the secret
Now that you are like nothing
But a shadow of a sound
Laughing from empty pillows
I want to understand you
I want to go on living

Who sat in this chair?
Who has drank with me?
Who rose from his pain
But did not leave it
Only to lay on tables
And never get up,
Keeps me in shadows
Neat and together
I will not ask; what is it?
Fall apart on your table
And I will keep your habit
In potted flowers
That say, I will remember
I will remember
Who sat in this chair
Who has drank with me

Now that you are dead
You will know what I'm saying
When I tell you I'm afraid
You were good for me
Now laughing hurts a little
When I tell you I'm afraid
You will know what I'm saying
Now that you are dead

Your voice is my dream
I carry it with some snow
Swept under a tree
Two ravens watch from
It is the sound of
Someone walking behind me
And the sound of not caring
And it's coming down
Not easy like sleep
Or what I won't understand
What if all the things you've said
Had a shadow still in love?
I'm feeling broken
Some things come out of a dream
But you have gone back
Hiding in the snow
Behind a wing in a tree

Now it seems to me
A second twilight
Came out of a scream
As if you had passed
With an un-natural light
This is your unborn invention
Or the meaning of a dream
Shaking the winter hour
It's what you wanted to say
Crying through the night
And so room was made
And in the morning
The snow was a veil
Of your un-opened torso

Echo is a bell
Wind is a service
Light is a broken window
Tiny bells of glass
Falling to the earth
Smaller than a dream
Whisper in the wind
And one day I will
Hear its invention
Together with the candles
In a midnight mass
I will say it's mine
Under closed eyes and cradles
I will say it's mine
Sleeping in my ear
Waiting behind the shadow
That could be a swan
When I say I blow them out
And scatter the eyes
Under a window
Fragile as eggshells
And I would go to sleep. For
In my dreams I walk
Through the broken glass

As a star is born
Or shadows when torn apart
Go without fear of falling
Because you have left
Glimmers of what could have been
Go without fear of falling
Or shadows when torn apart
As a star is born

The smell of snuffed wings
Doesn't remind you of snow
Or its hidden nest of fruit
It's not on the edge
Of seats waiting a last breath
It's not the words of lovers
Known by their lips or bound hands
It's not growing up
And forgetting lullabies
Or even giving your name
Just because the wind is there

III

I will not know if you will
Read what I have read
And recognize them
As having spaces
I left to tell you
It is what leaves you
When everything leaves
Between a word and a word
Someone talks for the first time
Someone falls in love
Someone believes they have dreamed
And I don't know if you will
In between two words
Forget that you must go on
In between two words
Tying a string to a branch
With missing snowflakes

You know those little spaces
Those little stars in the sky?
You know how something is said
And then said again?
Do you know their hands don't meet
Because they can fly?
And hearing someone believe
They were never lost
Smaller than a day
With tiny fingers
Trying to touch you
And then carry you away
Again and again
Little by little
Means nothing more than
When you hear someone believe
All the things you've said
And then said again
Dividing the night

Mirrors tell two lies
Nothing can be done
Nothing can be done
I have been waiting
To be something else
That goes unnoticed,
That has never known
The closed eyes of a cradle
Forgetting the earth
Can fall apart anytime
The overheard sound
Of forgotten hands
Waiting under every bed
Where no shadow falls
I've been waiting to tell you
I have my own lie—
I am nothing without it

I hear the shadows
Move into the sun
Although they cannot see me
Passing by windows
I turn to face them
Although they cannot see me
Move into the sun
I hear the shadows

Eating all the skin
My chains could offer
Eating each other
Putting on the weight of words
By feeling empty
In the spaces in between
Turning air into powder
We stuff ourselves with the dust
We're never taken away
And we are never returned
We are waiting for the wind
From the wings of startled birds
The closing of eyes
The sudden stillness
Of empty cradles
When no one's ready
They'll take it apart, and let
Children come out of our mouths
Some things belong in the wind
Some things should stay un-noticed
But it's not the same
When I say blow them away
Nothing can be done
I never grew up
I just grew over

If you have been here
Someone was set on fire
That is what happens
When you can no longer fly
Caught in the middle
It starts off like this
Abandoned children
That will see nothing
For a home in every hand
And close heaven's mouth
Because they can fall in love
It starts off like this
Now that they are lost
Beginnings and swallowed suns
Their bellies will fill with stars

What is twilight without me
Holding the bells of the sun
Behind my shoulder?
What is that familiar smell
Where I remember
Moment to moment
The clocks of unearthed flowers
Where wheels have faces of wheels
Timing every opened egg
Without a shelter of wings
Dying to wake up? But then
What am I without dying?

If sometimes there is a need
Not to feel guilty
Where should I begin?
I don't think you mean
I was ever lost, and that
It is not enough to lie
When heaven needs us
More than we need it
Just as I need you
More than you need me
How could I begin?
Maybe I should just go home
And think about you
Maybe just lying with me
Maybe just believing that
Why it doesn't have to take
More than children to save you

Sooner or later you'll know
Something in yourself
Speaks between the years
Dividing the night and day
Calling to the sun
That tears you away
Under the lamp light
Of what you won't understand
Because it is too pretty
And it seems too real
Now that you have passed through it
Blinded by the lack of sleep
Where hands lose their weight
Then, just fly away

This is the silence snow brings
When you hide yourself
Living moment to moment
You won't understand
Why you've come or why you'll go
Living moment to moment
When you hide yourself
This is the silence snow brings

I want you to be those stars
That sometimes winter's hour
Loose upon my sleeve
Lies still upon my table
What was shaken off
Maybe it's the years
Of broken mirrors
Where you were always
Trying to see behind them
Having no one to care for
Whatever they were
Had been forgotten
When you turned away
And then spent the night
Falling from the night
Smaller than a dream
You have never been missing
In what you can't take away
Maybe that's why I keep them
Tied with a string to a branch
I know you watch over me
I know you watch over me
When I can not sleep
Or forget why you
Must come together
When I fall apart

IV

I've never seen the ocean
Never stood upon its edge
Smaller than myself
And then whispered to the world
My un-gathered kiss
That had once meant everything
Larger than myself
Never meant to own
I've never seen the ocean
But I've waited under clouds
And held a hand
Smaller than myself
Wanting to count the first time
Falling in my heart
Drowning drop by drop
The sound of footsteps
That never arrive

Sometimes it is a ladder
Sometimes forgotten bottles
That must lead nowhere
Or be found broken
That should not carry
The weight of a crush
By single perfumes
Or conversations
And so shouldn't see
Or choose to be found
Leading to some place better
By what has been lost

Just a woman in a room
Looking at someone
Who refused to turn
But only motioned
As if opening a door
Returned a moment
Shut out from her heart
Leaving was all she could see
Though her eyes would run away
He would follow with his touch
And the silence of their words
Whispered tears in hands

They didn't know I was there
Or that I watched a phone ring
Though I couldn't count the hands
I saw something I shouldn't
I was out of place
I can sometimes tell people
Have their way with me
As I am getting younger
And it is almost enough
To just pick it up
And give it away
I will come and go
Even when I sleep
And what I keep around me
Doesn't answer when I call
Or even notice I'm there

I know I have hung somewhere
Alone in a tree
Leaning by windows
Waiting to be found
I have slept with the sidewalks
Feeling the weight of a crush
You only miss when you look
Feeling something has happened
An overheard voice
The fear of laughing
Waiting to be found
Before I can be
Undressed in my throat
Long after they have
Placed me on their lips

The emptied frames of pictures
Have the color of your hands
So that I am left again
Alone in your world
Of negative eyes
Where I have been terrible
And could only see
Everything that you were not
Coming from a place
Where you should have never been
Even though I knew your name
I couldn't say what it was
That was remembered
That was forgotten

Your angry words cannot tell
The empty cages of eyes
To close around them
They want to belong
When something opens
And forget themselves
In what you will fear
They want to be held
Because they can never be
And if you send them curses
Because you can no longer
Release them from what you hope
Then, like colors or cages
You will only hold yourself
Absent in your heart
By that which you give away

I see her in the women
But she never comes
Crowded by sidewalks
She has ungathered
Bodies upon me
Under waves of hands
It is hard to breath
Crying or laughing
Rising or falling
So many have come undone
Flooding my heart with panic
Which is never romantic
But only hangs from their clothes
As if by shipwrecks
She is stranded in their hair.

Wake up the thunder
Sunlight breaks on a tear
I have been with violence
And pressed flowers in her book
I have waited under smiles
That must sometimes sleep
Seeing the list of dead lights
Hiding their end with rainbows
Waiting to be touched
Wake up the thunder
And let it pass over me
I still want to see
When you are hungry
You bend in the light

The stillness of your body
Huddles with the rain
Your un-moving, un-closed eyes
Give away the violence
That you must have taken on
Calling it your own
Showing the world of hunger
The world of hunger
I cannot hold you
In anything that I need
But, I have waited for you
Behind the danger
In the struggle just to see
The waving away
In the figure of your smile
Quietly ruined

Leaning on my wall
There's a place to go
That is where you sleep
Resting against me
No longer afraid
That I will forget
Then I will show you
The angel sewn on my hip
And I will give back to you
The tired wings of my heart
That only flutter when caged
Forgetting how free
I was in your world
When you forget, someone else
Has remembered you
But, my forgetting is just
When you have remembered me

The world doesn't weigh on me
The way rainbows have
Sometimes the sky falls apart
And the sun breaks down
Hiding behind the thunder
And the world opens its world
And two bodies go static
And charge nothing but themselves
Hidden in whispers of air
They send out rumors
A trace of what was
Leaving you hungry
Never wanting to be blind
The world doesn't weigh on me
The way rainbows have
The way saying goodbye has
Knowing that you've turned away
Knowing you've been here

She was very young
With all the ways of a crush
She tried to see through
But there was hunger
Laying her on a table
Waiting to be found
So every hand brings a gift
But being willing
Has nothing to do with it
Her gift was her love
Never meant to be taken
Never meant to touch
His gift was a cage
Always meant for another
Always meant to own
Loose upon her hip
Where no one could see

V

They came down with the shadows
Un-earthed by the night
Showing me the wings
Missing from a child
And by luck I somehow saw
That I was afraid
To be a heaven
Of un-delivered cradles
And watch over them
I wanted to leave the world
Not because I saw
That I was afraid
But, because I remembered
Who they belonged to

Lay down your angels
Lay them down to sleep
Sweep the corners of their eyes
And leave a prayer on their lips
So many of the hour
That never ends are waiting
To confuse their dreams
In circles of smoke
And draw them out as
They draw themselves out
They can not be closed
As an eye or a spent flame
So lay them down with feathers
A piece of the night
An un-pinned shoulder

You will find them there
Those startled moments
Shaken from your bed
The mist of the night
Un-gathered upon your face
The whisper, the trace
Where something has fled
The terror of life
That you can not place
Calling from its cell
Cold as butterflies
Hollowed from their shell
You will find them there
Where everything ends

Behind every fear
There is a fear of falling
Where you hang by threads
If you believe there are dreams
Because the night has left you
Where you hang by threads
There is a fear of falling
Behind every fear

It is a circle
That closes into itself
Or opens into itself
It is a skeletons sigh
Or the scorched breath of angels
It is a broken mirror
That takes you apart
Or takes apart what you see
Starlight to sunlight
It divides the host
For some think that its beauty
And some think of suicide

Little shadow, little night
Little bird wounded by light
That which made you so afraid
Smoldering in you corner
Ready to conceive
That which made you so afraid
Little bird wounded by light
Little shadow, little night

Colder than the nails
Dead in a dead vein
There's a gathering of hands
Sending their chill down your neck
It is an ending
We can feel for them
As they are leaving someone
Lost or miss-understanding
And for a moment
We are shaken from the night
Lost or miss-understanding

There is a lost hand
That we hold onto
Where no sunlight breaks
Where no fire burns
Where a scream begins
By falling apart
We came together
Forever in the space
We can never see
Those, who un-tying themselves
Looking for the rest
Those, who hang by threads
Hanging by a fear
That are pieces of them
Or of us missing

You made a hole in your heart
So you could come out
Hoping to be lost
But only went on
As if re-living
The un-tying of yourself
Casting your broken pieces
In the corners of the night
A whisper of surrender
That murmurs with chills
And the damp fingerprints
Where the heave of chains
Wrench the flood of tears
The heavenly gate
That closes across your reach
And cradle the rest
You no longer feel
Until sunbeams bend
You voice and sling
Where you struggle with yourself
Not to have a dream
But to be a dream

You do not reflect
The gay lifting of twilight
Inside your restless cradle
No hearts or hammers
No laughter of arms
Play out their song of rising
Against your hollow
The eventide lays
Its torso like a raw nerve
Where you draw its life
Like a final breadth
that rent its bare thread
Into an endless
Shattering stillness

In a hollow hourglass
The sound of a butterfly
Remembered once more
The widows and hands
Those who lost and lost
Remembered once more
The sound of a butterfly
In a hollow hourglass

You left them for the sun rise
Covered in yourself
Un-veiled around them
Lost but not broken
You swallowed them whole
Lost within yourself
You smothered their wings
Wanting so much to be them
And for a moment
You came together
But, vacant is the hour
When you die before you wake
For sleep never ends
Hung for the sun rise
Lost within yourself

When they rise up from the earth
Holding the sky together
Un-gathering tiny wings
In constellations of night
Corner to corner
They flood the last home
They, who have nothing to loose
Without knowing what they've done
Remember nothing
As you lay them down to sleep
Remember nothing
That has yet to be un-done
Remember nothing
Remember nothing.